The Manager's Guide to Continuous Delivery

Delivering software in days,
instead of months

The Manager's Guide to Continuous Delivery
Delivering software in days, instead of months
First edition, first print, February 2014

Authors: Andrew Phillips, Michiel Sens,
Adriaan de Jonge, Mark van Holsteijn
Design: HGPDESiGN, Alphen aan den Rijn, www.hgpdesign.nl
Publisher: Uitgeverij TIEM, www.uitgeverijtiem.nl
ISBN/EAN: 978-90-79272-40-2

Table of Contents

Foreword by
Jeff Sutherland

Creator of Scrum

In this book the authors have done a fantastic job in capturing the complete overview of Continuous Delivery in a clear and understandable way. As an IT Manager this book will give you the insights and steps to get your organization to the next level. I recommend Continuous Delivery as the way to properly implement Scrum and as a mandatory cornerstone in the IT strategy of every successful agile company.

Let's face it. Most software projects are incredibly slow and have a staggering failure rate. Traditionally they use an outmoded methodology to make a big plan up front, then wait months to years to do final testing for something that is supposed to work, but usually does not. Even worse, technology moves too fast, the market changes and new leadership offers a new vision often before even one line of code can be written.

Let me give you an example. A couple of years ago the FBI spent 400 million dollars and three years with hundreds of people on a new software system. The system was useless so the Government Accounting Office sent Lockheed a cease and desist letter to terminate the project. Then something amazing happened. The FBI hired an agile CIO and CTO who moved into the basement of the FBI building with 15 developers and delivered the same project for less than 10% of the original budget in a little over a year. So for 10% of the cost and 15 times faster they delivered a system that actually worked and the users liked it.

This incredible turn-around success was achieved because of Scrum. Using Scrum the FBI delivered working software every few weeks and fully testing the system feature by feature as it was built. Scrum is the art of doing twice the work in half the time. It uses a simple framework that enhances innovation and collaboration by simplifying how people communicate. Across the world, organizations such as SAP, large financials and high-tech startups alike are switching over to Scrum so that they can deliver working software every few weeks.

However, at leading commercial software companies even delivering working software every few weeks is considered too slow. Consider Ancestry.com, which delivers 220 releases every two weeks. Or Hubspot.com, which delivers 170 live changes every day on a slow day. Or Google, which has 15,000 developers working on one branch of code that changes 20 times a minute! They are fast, incredibly fast.

The good news is that this speed is attainable for all organizations that take Scrum seriously. The secret of teams delivering at this speed is that they continuously implement better engineering practices, sprint after sprint, as part of the continuous improvement practice built into Scrum. These engineering practices ensure the capability to go live flawlessly, many times per day, with impeccable quality.

Continuous Delivery captures the sum and wisdom of the best engineering practices in the industry as a total concept. Using Continuous Delivery practices is the future for every agile team. Proper Scrum teams first deliver working software every few weeks and as they use Continuous Delivery practices to aggressively work on better results, many find they can deliver a new product release every day, or even multiple times per day.

In this book the authors have done a fantastic job in capturing the complete overview of Continuous Delivery in a clear and understandable way. As an IT Manager this book will give you the insights and steps to get your organization to the next level. I recommend Continuous Delivery as the way to properly implement Scrum and as a mandatory cornerstone in the IT strategy of every successful agile company.

Jeff Sutherland, Ph.D.
MIT Cambridge Innovation Center, 2014

Foreword by David Farley

Co-author of Continuous Delivery, Reliable Software Releases through Build, Test, and Deployment Automation

> Continuous Delivery is the most effective approach to developing high quality software that we have found so far. This is the process that some of the most successful companies in the world now use to gain market advantage.

Continuous Delivery is at the leading edge of software development thinking. Most of the literature and discussion focuses on the technical aspects, but this is a process that crosses boundaries and helps to make businesses more efficient. This book is aimed at the business person who wants to understand the Continuous Delivery approach.

Software development is an extremely difficult undertaking. Software is unlike most endeavours with which we are familiar. Creating software is a technically demanding process. It often demands advanced problem solving techniques and high levels of creativity. On top of all of that, software is remarkably fragile, a tiny error, one wrong character in the equivalent of a chapter, is enough to prevent it from working.

As a result of these demands, the software industry has often struggled to effectively meet the needs of the businesses that it serves. It has been far too common for software development projects to be late, deliver poor quality and deliver software that doesn't meet the needs of it's users. There have been many attempts to tackle this problem, but over the past few years there has been a significant change. Learning from the scientific method, advanced quality-focussed processes and experiments in software development process we have evolved techniques that we can finally claim, with some authority, work.

Continuous Delivery is the most effective approach to developing high quality software that we have found so far. This is the process that some of the most successful companies in the world now use to gain market advantage. The early adopters were web companies, including some of the largest and most successful, but increasingly this process is now being adopted in all types of organisation, developing all kinds of software and in widely different business sectors. This adoption is happening because this process works! Businesses that have adopted Continuous Delivery are more successful as a result. They get higher-quality software into the hands of their users and customers faster than before and so can react to business demand and change more rapidly.

Continuous Delivery works because it depends on a more scientific approach to development. We attempt to establish feedback mechanisms that show the results of our work more quickly. We aim to make our software more verifiable at all levels.

Continuous Delivery changes the way that you and your software development teams work together, this is not a process that stops at the boundaries of the software development team. It helps to foster a professional, high-performance team culture. It frees each group to make the professional decisions for which they are trained and yet encourages them to interact more and depend upon one another's skills and expertise.

I believe that in any market, a company that uses Continuous Delivery for software development has a significant advantage over those that don't. This is not because of the technicalities, but because it provides a business the freedom to experiment and so to react to change. If you work for a company that relies on software development these changes are going to affect you. If you adopt them they will change the way that you work, and improve the efficiency, effectiveness and quality of your software and your business. If you don't you will see increasing competition from those that do.

I hope you enjoy this book, and I hope that you enjoy the process of discovery and the sense of teamwork that adopting Continuous Delivery so often initiates.

Dave Farley

1

Introduction

Turning good ideas into marketable features quickly is a business imperative for every enterprise. Getting features "out there" faster and at high levels of quality is the first critical step. The subsequent step is to rapidly collect feedback from your users in order to guide your next set of ideas.

First, deliver features better. Then, deliver better features better!

Continuous Delivery is a set of processes and practices that radically removes waste from your software production process, enables a faster delivery of high-quality functionality and sets up a rapid and effective feedback loop between your business and your users. In a competitive economic environment, every organization should at least consider this game-changing approach.

Continuous Delivery will help you reduce your time to market from weeks and months to days or hours!

2

Meet Ostrich Insurance, the Traditional Company

Continuous Delivery promises to deliver new features to production in a matter of hours. In this chapter, we illustrate the problems that exist in a traditional software delivery process where this often takes many months.

In order to properly motivate the practices and processes of Continuous Delivery, we first look at the manner in which software functionality is delivered in a traditional organization: Ostrich Insurance.

Ostrich is a traditional company that has been doing things a certain way for a long time. To remain competitive in the insurance market, Ostrich shifted to selling their products online a while ago. However, it is hard for them to compete in the online market, because it simply takes them too much time to deliver new software.

Communication between business, development, QA and operations takes place on many different levels and often leads to confusion. Handoffs between the different groups involved in the overall process introduce long waiting times and provide yet further opportunity for hesitation and disruption.

Slow, error-prone, manual processes, delays, handoffs and lengthy fix cycles inevitably lead to infrequent releases. And when you infrequently release large numbers of changes and fixes in one go, the go-live is predestined to be stressful and often followed by days or weeks of post-release emergency patches.

How can the business ever release features quickly and reliably under these circumstances?

In order to help identify Ostrich's challenges, let us look at the value stream map for their software delivery process – a proven technique for identifying and progressively eliminating waste in a process.

0. Requirements: We Know Everything

Conditioned to work with large, infrequent releases, the business analyst tries to specify the complete feature set up front. To try to avoid ambiguity and differences in interpretation, he creates very detailed descriptions in an attempt to capture all use cases and scenarios the business can imagine. Inevitably, this involves second-guessing the details of what customers *actually* want, leading to many features that end up not quite meeting their expectations.

It also means that, from the perspective of delivering business value, there is already a built-in time-to-market delay, because sufficient features need to be gathered before work on a single feature can even start.

Duration: weeks to months
Waste: Wrong features specified; features not specified correctly; features specified at an excessive level of detail; no customer feedback cycle in large up-front product design; no advice from developers to design for feasibility

1. Coding: Postponing Problems

The specifications of the feature requirements are passed to one or more development teams one by one. Developers work in isolation, each making changes to their copy of the application code without being aware of any possible overlapping changes made by their colleagues. After several weeks, work that is related to a particular feature is complete.

Duration: several weeks
Waste: Duplicated effort; lack of communication between the developers

2. Integrating: Merge Hell

After weeks of working on an isolated copy of the codebase, the new features now need to be combined (this is called *merging*) into one single codebase. The longer the team waits with merging the code and the larger the development team, the greater the number of conflicting changes that need to be handled. Late and infrequent integration is a very typical recipe for missing deadlines and introduces significant risk.

> **Duration:** days
> **Waste:** Conflict resolution during merging; problem needs to be solved by the entire team

3. Installing: Error-prone Manual Deployment

After weeks of manually tweaking the development machines in order to get the application to run, the development team now needs to prepare an installation manual to allow operations to deploy the new version to the subsequent test environments as well. This installation manual usually describes all the steps that the developers *remember*, but it certainly does *not* describe a fully tested procedure.

The installation manual and application binaries are handed off to operations via a shared network drive. A support ticket is created for operations to deploy the application to the test environment in the next available timeslot.

Just before the deadline of the service level agreement for handling the support ticket expires, the request is picked up by an operator, who attempts to deploy the application according to the manual. After a couple of steps, the operator runs into an error, adds a comment to the ticket and passes it back to the development team.

The next morning, the QA team that is expecting to start a test cycle discovers that the application isn't even running. The lead developer checks the support ticket, discovers a typo in the installation manual, uploads a new manual to the network share (obscuring the audit trail in the process) and hands the ticket back to operations.

Eventually, the operator resumes work on the ticket and finally completes the installation.

Duration: 1 week

Waste: Waiting for deployment to be carried out; fixing incorrect deployment instructions; fixing incorrect deployments; waiting for target environment to become available; QA waiting for application to test to become available; "Ping-pong" between different teams

4. Testing: Lowering The Bar after Manual QA

The QA team can now start their acceptance test. During the development phase, the team translated the detailed business requirements into extensive test plans. Some of the requirements seem to be good candidates for the test automation tool used at Ostrich. For these type of requirements, the team tried to translate requirement descriptions into automation scripts that the tool is able to run. Like all translations, this is a challenging process resulting in a number of requirements incorrectly or insufficiently covered by automated tests.

The lengthy process of executing the test plan gets underway. On completion, the QA team prepares its report, which identifies 15 failing test scenarios – enough for the release to be put on hold. With many important features threatening to be delayed by the 15 failing tests and pressure from the business mounting, it is decided that only 3 of the defects are indeed show stoppers that *really* need to be fixed before continuing. A patch is quickly rushed out, the 3 scenarios are verified, and the updated version is reluctantly passed by the QA team.

The release manager now creates a support ticket to release the patched version to production, accepting the fact that 12 of the requirements originally laid out failed the test! These will need to be addressed in an urgent maintenance release that is now planned in a hurry.

Duration: 3 weeks
Waste: Translation of requirements into tests; waiting for test completion before fixing; developing features that do not work; testing scenarios that are determined to be non-essential; many correct features waiting for 3 defects to be fixed; miscommunication caused by differing interpretation of requirements; handoffs between different teams

5. Release Preparation: The Pre-Production Bottleneck

Before the new version can be released to production, it must pass a final set of tests in the pre-production environment. This is required to increase the confidence level that the go-live will succeed, since the acceptance environment differs quite substantially from production. Getting an exclusive slot for the busy pre-production environments has to be planned well in advance; this time, the next available slot is two weeks down the line.

Once the application is installed in the pre-production environment, the QA team starts the production integration, stability and regression tests. After a week, the team finds two errors,

which are fixed by the development team two days later.
After a short retest of the failed scenarios, the release is accepted
for production.

Duration: 4 weeks
Waste: waiting for the pre-production environment to become
available; missed deadlines; errors found late in the process

6. Go-Live: The Quarterly Release Cycle

The new application version has been approved just in time for
the next available quarterly release slot, coming up in 3 weeks.
As usual, it will be busy and stressful: from Saturday night to
Sunday, Operations is supposed to manually deploy 9 new application versions. After 4 hours of manually executing the installation
steps described in the various manuals, the QA department takes
another 4.5 hours to verify the releases. Just before the go/no-go
deadline is reached, QA completes testing, and with many sighs
of relief the application is live.

Duration: 3 weeks
Waste: waiting for the release window; out-of-hours work

In short, from a business perspective: it has taken months to get
only a small subset of the features Ostrich *thinks* their customers
need into production. Important fixes are outstanding, and it will
be difficult or impossible for Ostrich to gauge the impact of each
of the new features in order to address their customers' needs
better in future.

Key learning points

A traditional software delivery process prevents your from responding to your customers' needs quickly and reliably:

- Individual features or requests cannot be quickly implemented
- Delivery process is slow, unreliable and error-prone
- Quality levels are low due to late discovery of errors

3

Meet the Competitor:
Future Insurance

In the previous chapter, we saw how a traditional
software delivery process prevents organizations from
reacting quickly and reliably to market demand. In this
chapter, we illustrate how Continuous Delivery enables
the rapid delivery of high quality features to production.

Let us compare the situation at Ostrich with that of its competitor, Future Insurance. Looking at market developments, they acknowledged early that it was no longer acceptable to deliver new products or update product features at the same pace at which they had been operating for the past ten years.

Future Insurance examined its software delivery value stream and pinpointed every step in the process that was costly, time-consuming or prone to errors. They removed, automated or accelerated every single step, until they had put in place a rapid, cost-efficient and reliable process. This transition was based on the practices and principles of Continuous Delivery.

At Future Insurance, the feedback cycle between the business and the end user is incredibly tight, enabling a rapid "dialogue" with customers that ensures each idea and feature delivered is aligned with the current needs and wishes of Future Insurance's. For Future Insurance, it's not just about delivering ideas faster and more efficiently. It's about enabling the business to reliably have better, more relevant and more timely ideas *in the first place*. The differences between Future Insurance and Ostrich go beyond just the development process: the business does not attempt to dream up new features based on a guess of what users might like.

Instead, they identify improvements based on analysis of user responses by looking at user interaction data, system metrics, social media output and comparisons with groups of users exposed to a different subset of features. Based on this analysis the business, which constantly keeps track of customer behavior through live dashboards and visualizations, decides to try out new features.

0. Collaborating: End-to-end Feature Teams

At Future Insurance, new ideas are formulated and prepared
for inclusion in the delivery stream by an end-to-end team that
involves all relevant groups as soon as possible: business analysts,
developers, testers and operators. This approach ensures that
everybody has a shared understanding of an idea and will be able
to implement this idea effectively. This agile team covers the
entire spectrum of service delivery and is involved in making the
product a success at every step of the way.

1. Defining: Specifications Become Automated Acceptance Tests

No matter how agile or lean you are, a change should be specified
before it is implemented. In contrast to the lengthy documents
common at Ostrich, specs at Future Insurance are formulated
by the entire delivery team, with primarily the business and
QA working together to write executable tests in business-level
language. This increases efficiency and eliminates a source of
miscommunication in one stroke: why first write a specification
on paper and later request someone else to translate it into code
for a test tool, when both people can work together to define a
single executable test in one step?

Duration: 0.5 day

1. Coding: Tests First, Then Code

Before a developer at Future Insurance starts implementing a
feature, it writes a failing unit test for the piece of code about to be
written. Only then does the developer start writing code to make the
test succeed. This practice, which is followed by all other developers
working on the application, has resulted in a large body of unit tests
validating that all the pieces of code continue to behave as intended.

Since all these unit tests still pass after the new code has been added, the change is checked into version control. By doing so, the change is added to the same codebase being worked on by all other developers on the team. The updated codebase is now verified *again* by the Continuous Integration server to check that the new code does not conflict with changes made by other developers. If this build fails, the entire team is immediately notified, and correcting the mistake to "get the build back to green" becomes the top priority for the team. Any member of the team can fix, or even simply remove, the new change to correct the mistake in minutes.

Duration: 0.5 day

2. Off It Goes: the Continuous Delivery Pipeline

The integration build is the first step a new feature takes on its journey through the continuous delivery pipeline. We will verify that the feature not only passes the automated acceptance test that is our specification, but also meets system requirements for security, performance, availability etc.

These tests are carried out in automated, "hands-off" environments: test systems which are created and torn-down as needed, without human intervention. Our feature is automatically deployed onto these environments, after which applicable tests are immediately executed.

The speed and reliability of automatically provisioning and configuring the production-like test environments is critical to the pipeline. It allows Future Insurance to accelerate throughput by performing many types of tests in parallel adding to the confidence that results of high quality will carry over to production.

Most important, the status of each feature in the pipeline is immediately visible, and progress is highly predictable at all times. Everyone involved in feature delivery – from the business and development to QA and operations – has complete visibility every step of the way.

Duration: 0.5 day

3. Go-live: The Product Owner Hits the Button

When a new feature did not cause any failures in the pipeline, the business owner is notified and asked to approve the new version of the application. This is mostly a formality as the feature has already passed thousands of automated tests which ran overnight. All tests results are summarized in a quality dashboard for review and drill-down if desired.

By approving the new feature, the business owner adds it to the next fully automated production deployment. These deployments take place at regular intervals around the clock, with no developer or operator required. Deploying a new feature is as easy as publishing an article in a content management system.

For many applications at Future Insurance, the business trusts the tests to the point that any feature that makes it through the pipeline is approved. After all, any new change is initially only exposed to a percentage of the customer base. If significant problems are detected in this "canary" subset, the change is automatically rolled back.

Duration: 1 hour

This approach allows the business to concentrate on reacting quickly and responsively to user input to devise the next "killer feature" that will take Future Insurance even further ahead of their competitors.

Key learning points

Continuous Delivery enables the rapid delivery of high quality features to production, allowing the business and IT to work together to react quickly to the demands of customers and outpace the competition.

- Multi-disciplinary, end-to-end feature team involved from the beginning.
- Visibility into progress and quality levels throughout the process.
- Reliable delivery through an automated build, deployment, test and release process.
- Instant user feedback on new features continuously monitored by the business.

4

The Role of
the Business

In the previous chapter, we saw how Continuous
Delivery enables rapid delivery of high quality features
to your users. In this chapter, we stress the importance
of buy-in and committed involvement in the delivery
process by the business.

One of the key appeals of Continuous Delivery is that it gives the business much more direct control of feature development – from "throwing a bunch of the requirements over the wall to IT and waiting months to see what comes out" to "having an idea today and being able to follow all its steps to go-live tomorrow".

Putting the business behind the wheel is an important step. However, in order to make Continuous Delivery a success, the business also needs to keep its eyes firmly on the road and concentrate on the journey. The business needs to be prepared to commit full-time resources – dedicated Product Owners – to gather and evaluate feedback from the user community and work with testers and developers to refine new features and improvements and define specifications in the form of automated acceptance tests.

In an effective Continuous Delivery environment, the ability of the pipeline to churn out new functionality can be so significant, that simply ensuring that enough new features and ideas are ready to be worked on can become a challenging task.

In order to get the most out of Continuous Delivery, we have to ensure the business itself does not become the bottleneck. Early expectation management and communication of the new responsibilities to the business are essential to realizing the potential of Continuous Delivery. If not addressed properly, we risk ending up with an idling racecar.

Key learning point

A successful Continuous Delivery implementation depends on buy-in across the organization. Continuous Delivery puts the business in more direct control of the delivery process but requires committed, on-going involvement.

5

An Introduction to the Continuous Delivery Pipeline

In the previous chapter, we stressed the importance of
the committed involvement of the whole organization
in the Continuous Delivery process. In this chapter, we
describe the delivery pipeline: the key concept driving
the continuous flow of changes to production.

The goal of Continuous Delivery is to create a constant flow of changes to production: an automated software production line. The core concept that makes this happen is the Continuous Delivery pipeline. The pipeline breaks the software delivery process down into a number of stages. Each stage is aimed at verifying quality of new features from a different angle in order to prevent errors from affecting your users.

The pipeline should provide feedback to the team and visibility into the flow of changes to everyone involved in feature delivery. A typical Continuous Delivery pipeline can be broken down into the following stages:

0. The initial stages: Build automation and Continuous Integration

The pipeline starts by building the binaries to create the deliverable(s) that will be passed to the subsequent stages. New features implemented by the developers are integrated in the central code base on a continuous basis, built and unit tested. This is the most direct feedback cycle that tells the development team about the "health" of their application code.

1. The verification stages: Test automation

Subsequent stages in the pipeline ensure that all desired system qualities are met by the new version of the application. It is important that all relevant aspects – whether functionality, security, performance or compliance – are verified by the pipeline. The stages may involve different types of automated or (initially, at least) manual activities, or require human authorization.

2. The rollout stage: Deployment automation

The final stage of the pipeline is deployment to production. Since the preceding stages have verified the overall quality of the system, this is now a low-risk step. The deployment can be staged, with the new version being initially released to a subset of the production environment and monitored before being completely rolled out. The deployment is automated, allowing for reliable delivery of new functionality to users within minutes whenever this is needed.

3. Foundations: Platform provisioning
The deployment pipeline is supported by platform provisioning and system configuration management, which allows teams to create, maintain and tear-down complete environments automatically or at the push of a button. Automated platform provisioning ensures that all tests are carried out against correctly configured and reproducible environments. It also facilitates horizontal scalability and allows the business to try out new products in a sandbox environment at any time.

4. Orchestrating it all: Release coordination
The multiple stages in a deployment pipeline will involve different groups of people collaborating and supervising the release of the new version of your application. Release coordination provides a top-level view of the entire pipeline, allowing you to define and control the stages and gain insight into the overall software delivery process.

Analyzing this value stream highlights any remaining inefficiencies and hot-spots and pinpoints opportunities for further optimization of your pipeline.

Don't add new functionality before quality is right!
Continuous Delivery is about enabling your organization to bring new features to production, one by one, quickly and reliably. That means that every individual feature needs to be seen through to completion, meeting the quality requirements set for the overall system.

In a traditional environment, development teams try to implement an entire new version in one go, intending to address software quality characteristics such as robustness, extensibility, maintainability etc. only once the project is close to completion.

In consequence, the software only reaches a state suitable for shipping to the customer at the very end of the project, and thus delivering business value at the very end of the project! As deadlines loom and budget pressure grows, quality is often the first thing that is compromised.

Poor system quality, low user satisfaction and endless "quality band-aids" can be avoided by adopting the principle of not adding new functionality before "quality is right". You should always first meet and maintain your quality levels and only then consider gradually adding functionality to the system.

Quality = Functionality (what the system does) * System Qualities (how well it does it)

With Continuous Delivery, each new feature is required to meet the level of quality expected for the system as a whole, right from the start. Only once this quality level has been reached this feature can be moved to production.

Key learning points

The delivery pipeline is the key concept that enables a continuous flow of changes to production in a Continuous Delivery environment. Key points of the pipeline are:

- Functionality is only added when the quality is right.
- All changes to the source code immediately result in a new version of the application.
- Each new version is automatically tested against all available tests.
- New versions are automatically deployed to production.
- All installation and configuration of machines and environments is fully automated.

6

Test: Move the Tests Up Front

In the previous chapter, we introduced the delivery pipeline as the key concept enabling a continuous flow of changes to production. In this chapter, we show how the pipeline guarantees high levels of quality.

The standard approach to testing is to first develop new features, and then to test them. As a result, testing becomes a roadblock that stands in the way of go-live. After all, "the code is already there – what are we waiting for?" Inevitable delays result in testing being cut short, resulting in the low quality of many released features.

In a Continuous Delivery environment, we adopt a more productive approach. With automatically testable specifications, testing becomes the *first* thing we do, *before* development starts. Automating our tests allows testing to be a continuous activity that is performed continuously within the development process. Moving to this model provides a real-time picture of the current level of functionality and quality at all stages in the delivery pipeline.

Executable Specifications: Automated Acceptance Testing

Traditional specifications are dustware: they disappear into a desk drawer and quickly become obsolete as requirements and functionality change. These lengthy documents first need to be translated into test cases, which are then usually executed manually: a costly, time-consuming process which frequently results in tests that do not actually verify the originally intended functionality in the first place.

In a Continuous Delivery setup, we can switch to executable specifications. These are formulated using a structured natural language which can be read and understood by both the business and the test tool. No more "lost in translation" problems: the specification *is* the functional acceptance test!

Automated functional acceptance tests perform *black box testing*, in which the internals of the system are not known. They approach the system from a user's point of view, and so also function as automated acceptance criteria.

They are automatically evaluated as features move through the delivery pipeline, allowing us to track the progress of development in real time.

There's More to Quality Than Functionality: Automated Non-Functional Testing

Implementing a piece of functionality that works under "friendly circumstances", such as on a developer's laptop, is relatively simple. Writing high quality software for the real world, at acceptable cost, is a much bigger challenge.

As with functional specifications, we need to start by identifying our quality requirements, and state them in a testable – ideally, *automatically* testable – form. In a Continuous Delivery environment, it's important to remember that non-functional requirements can be part of the feedback loop just as much as feature ideas: system metrics such as latency, load and stability can equally give rise to new improvements.

Treating non-functional improvements as "just another type of change" is also a good way to find a balance between functionals and non-functionals, which all contribute to overall system quality. Non-functional requirements tend to be overlooked by the business, while developers can have a tendency to focus on them too strongly.

It is important to internally agree that improvement items can be placed on the backlog by developers and testers, and not just by the business owner. Using data about system performance and user experience allow architectural improvements and other changes that tackle "technical debt" to be prioritized more fairly. They can then be handled by the Continuous Delivery pipeline in the same manner as a new feature.

When writing your acceptance criteria, make sure you include non-functional requirements as part of the overall quality specification. Once these requirements are known, test for them! Automate these tests and run them often.

Keeping The System Running: Automated Regression Testing

In order to successfully implement Continuous Delivery, we need a high degree of confidence that we can deliver new features quickly and regularly *without breaking existing functionality*. Such errors are called *regressions* and, especially if they affect frequently-used or highly visible parts of the system, will quickly result in a poor user experience.

A very useful type of testing when it comes to preventing regressions caused by the small, incremental changes Continuous Delivery aims for, is testing of the internals, or *white box testing*. In software development, testing the behavior of a piece of code by itself is called *unit testing*. In Test Driven Development, the developer writes unit tests *before* writing the actual code. These tests thus serve as a description *and* verification of intended behavior. Once a unit test is created, it is run every time, safeguarding the ongoing correct functioning of this component.

This growing body of unit tests is invaluable in helping ensure all the pieces of the system still work as intended as we introduce changes, either to add functionality and especially when restructuring the system to improve non-functional qualities.

Avoiding regressions through extensive automated testing is a key part of a successful Continuous Delivery pipeline. Many types of regression testing will be required, since we want to ensure that all system qualities, from functionality to performance to reliability, remain stable. But of course we also can't afford to run all our automated tests for every single commit, as the required throughput time can quickly run into hours and days.

From a manager's perspective, good regression tests are determined by two measures: coverage and execution time. Coverage is a *percentage* that indicates how much of the system's behavior is validated by the tests. Aim for 100% but make sure that the tests are meaningful and relevant, verifying especially those parts of the system that will result in the greatest loss in business value if regressions occur. Aim also to keep the time required to run each test as low as possible – otherwise, we may achieve 100% coverage but will simply not have the time to run our tests.

Overall, a balance needs to be found between the maximum acceptable runtime for tests and the degree of coverage achievable. We can also use a tiered approach, with tests covering highly critical parts of our applications being executed for every change, while having the full test set run less frequently.
In order to minimize the need for this tradeoff, you should optimize your test infrastructure and tooling, and make use of any opportunity to run tests in parallel.

Key learning points

Before we can speed up the delivery process, we need to make sure that the quality of the software is guaranteed.

- Testing takes priority over developing code.
- Automated acceptance tests are written with the business to verify new functionality.
- Automated tests for non-functional requirements are included in the process.
- Automated regression tests ensure the system remains stable.

7

Development:
Instant Visibility

In the previous chapter, we saw how Continuous Delivery focuses on tests before writing code to guarantee quality. In this chapter, we show how Continuous Delivery provides fast feedback and instant visibility during development to delivery high quality code.

In a traditional software development organization, developers often work in isolation until, every couple of weeks or months, an attempt is made to merge all changes into central version control and "build the whole thing". Getting this to work takes a lot of effort and is a significant source of frustration. In such a process, developers spend a lot of time getting all parts of the code to work together, instead of focusing on creating tangible improvements and value for end users.

With Continuous Delivery, developers commit their changes to central version control several times a day, from where the changes are automatically built and tested to produce an updated version of the product. The application is always "ready to go", allowing the team to focus on functionality and delivering high quality features to customers.

Once executable specifications describing what needs to be built are in place, it is time to develop the code to implement the desired functionality.

In a Continuous Delivery environment, we make use of a number of tools and practices that focus on ensuring that each new feature works in the context of the overall system: Test Driven Development, Continuous Integration and product dashboards are all about identifying errors and defects as early as possible and making them clearly visible. After all, problems found at this stage of the delivery process are still relatively easily and quickly fixed.

Test Driven Development – First the test, then the code

A developer should only be writing code required to ensure the new feature meets specifications. If the code needs to be modified later, for instance in case the functionality needs to be extended, or to improve maintainability or performance, the developer also needs to make sure that such changes do not break anything else. These challenges are addressed by writing code-level tests before writing the actual program code, a practice called Test Driven Development. The developer starts by writing failing "unit tests" for each a component, or "unit", of the new feature. Code implementing the feature is then added until these tests all pass. The result of the unit tests makes the progress of the implementation of a feature clearly visible.

The updated code can then be committed to version control, where Continuous Integration takes over to verify that the new version of the system as a whole meets the business requirements and desired quality levels.

Continuous Integration – Nobody goes home if the build is broken

Your software developers deliver business value through working software. For software to work, it must first build. Building your application on a regular basis forces the development teams to ensure all the various components fit together at any moment in time.

The most effective way to ensure code is regularly assembled is to maintain a central Build and Continuous Integration server. This automatically tries to run a new build on a "clean" system whenever the code in the central version control system is changed. When the build succeeds, the team's build dashboard stays green. If the build fails, it turns red.

Before leaving the office, any developer that has added a code change to version control needs to wait until the Build & CI server has successfully verified the updated code. If the build fails and the dashboard goes red, the developer has two options:

1. Fix the error
2. Remove the change and return to the last working version

The ability to roll back the change means that no developer should need to leave the office with the application in a "broken" state, which would block the progress of the rest of the development team.

Dashboards – It's all about quality

In a large software project, it's easy enough to hide flaws. Code bases can stretch to millions of lines of code, with quality rarely being checked. Developers themselves quickly get used to "smell" in the code and stop noticing it.

Many automated tools are available that can make flaws in code visible. Insufficient test coverage, failing tests or complex, unmaintainable code: they can all be identified automatically. Usage of such tools is essential since achieving and maintaining a high level of build quality requires dedication and constant attention beyond the human capacity of most teams.

Under pressure of deadlines, relaxing quality standards "for a short while" sounds like a just-about-feasible option. The problem is that, in the long run, the cost of maintaining and enhancing a system with low levels of code quality, by far exceeds the short-term time gain. Continuous Delivery quickly makes it apparent that it is possible to maintain high software quality and quickly and reliably deliver software that runs well.

To ensure that quality is never sacrificed, the team should set quality standards and adhere to them at all times. Builds should always finish with at least an automated run of static tests, component (or unit) tests and functional tests. The results should become clearly visible on a large screen in the teams' working areas.

High visibility of build results showcase achievement and foster a sense pride – this is not about punishment and finger pointing. It is about demonstrating to all, including the business, that your team really is able to deliver high quality software. A product version should be eligible for release only when the agreed quality standards have been met.

Take build infrastructure seriously

If your build server's capacity is saturated and teams are waiting for builds to start, or if the server cannot be restored after a crash because no backups are available, your ability to deliver new features is impaired. Treat your build and test servers as a critical part of your delivery infrastructure which needs to scalable, properly maintained and backed up on a regular basis.

No builds or broken builds mean no new features for your customers and no generation of business value.

Key learning points

Continuous Delivery ensures development results in a high-quality product that is releasable at any moment by:

- Applying Test Driven Development: Tests are written before the code.
- Continuously integrating all changes made by all developers, ensuring the resulting application version works.
- Providing instant visibility into the quality of the software through prominent dashboards.
- Having a robust, performant and scalable build and test infrastructure.

8

Deployment:
Make it a Non-event

In the previous chapter, we saw how Continuous Delivery
provides fast feedback during the development process
and ensures your applications are always ready for
release. In this chapter, we show how Continuous
Delivery takes the pain out of getting a new application
version to production.

In a traditional environment, the deployment of a new version of the application to an environment is a time-consuming and error-prone process. The development team puts together a deployment package, prepares a manual and hands the whole thing off to operations for the actual execution. Slight differences between the configurations of each environment frequently cause deployments to fail and result in even more delays and idle time. Deploying to production is an extremely stressful exercise where organisations tend to postpone it for as long as possible.

With Continuous Delivery, new application versions are automatically deployed in a matter of minutes, providing instant feedback to the delivery team allowing them to respond rapidly to customer demand. Deploying to production is a routine non-event that occurs multiple times a day. Additional deployment strategies such as canary releasing allow new features to be exposed to a small set of customers to monitor whether they are functional and effective – both technically and commercially -, before exposing the features to the complete user base.

Deploy anytime, anywhere

In traditional IT organizations, the deployment of a new application is a highly bureaucratic, often manual process. Deploying a new version to a target environment is so time-consuming and mired in red tape that development teams avoid it for as long as they can. When the paperwork has finally been dealt with, it still takes a lot of time and technical effort on the part of both development and operations to actually get the new version up and running.

In a Continuous Delivery scenario, the deployment process across all target environments is fully automated, allowing the organization to quickly test new functionality in any environment and deploy new versions to production on demand. Automating the deployment process helps bridge the gap between development and operations and build end-to-end delivery teams. An automated deployment process should be a standard project deliverable from day one, with development and operations jointly determining and implementing an automated strategy to ensure that deployments "just work".

Since deployments are carried out frequently as an application moves through the delivery pipeline, the deployment process itself is tested every time a code change triggers a new pipeline run. Problems in the deployment configuration are quickly highlighted, and can be fixed in the same manner and at the same time as problems in the application code.

It should be possible for any team member with sufficient authorization, including the business owner, to initiate a deployment to any of the target environments with a simple click, eliminating dependencies on operations or even specific operators. By automating deployments, the reproducibility of deployments is guaranteed while the deployment server itself maintains a full audit trail for each and every deployment.

Removing manual steps and hand-offs from the deployment process significantly reduces throughput time, the number of failures and troubleshooting sessions and, in consequence, the overall cost of software delivery.

Test it in production – Canary releases and Dark launches

In a traditional software delivery process, a lot of manual effort goes into testing a new application version as thoroughly as possible before it is approved for production. Problems that surface after the go-live cause the organisation to add yet further checks and tests into the release process, lengthening the time to market even more.

With Continuous Delivery, the release of a feature to production is an uneventful experience. Using *canary releases* and *dark launches*, an incremental deployment strategy is applied that minimizes the risk of downtime and allows the delivery team to discover how the application behaves in a production environment without immediately impacting all users. The insight into real-life customer behavior enables the organization to learn faster and make better business decisions, day after day.

In a *canary release*, the new application version is deployed to only a small number of servers in production, running side by side with the existing version. A percentage of the systems' users is directed to the new "trial" version, where the behavior of the users and system is closely monitored. Any anomalies are quickly detected without affecting the vast majority of customers.

When necessary, the sample users can instantly be redirected back to the stable version, and the "canary servers" rolled back to the prior version with a single click using deployment automation. If all goes well, the new version is rolled out to the entire production environment.

With *dark launches*, new application versions and features are deployed to production without being made directly visible to users. Runtime options in the software (feature flags) allow you to expose specific features to a controlled subset of your user base, usually an "early access" group: employees, partner companies or "friends & family". Dark launches can also be used to put new features in production without users noticing. For example, a feature may not yet be visible in the user interface, but the underlying code can already be running, allowing results to be analyzed.

In short, the main purpose of canary releases is to further reduce the risk of production releases. Dark launches are an effective strategy to silently observe the impact of new functionality on the system "in the real world", and to carry out A/B testing by selectively providing different sets of functionality to subsets of your user base.

Key learning points

In a Continuous Delivery environment, moving a new version through the pipeline and deploying it to production becomes a "non-event".

- No more handoffs between development and operations.
- Deployment of new versions of the software to all environments is fully automated.
- Features can be deployed incrementally to production and exposed to users gradually.
- Tests can be carried out against "silent" features in production to measure the quality and impact of changes.

9

Provisioning:
Pipeline Foundations

In the previous chapter, we saw how moving a new version through the pipeline and deploying it to production becomes a non-event. In this chapter, we show how automated provisioning and middleware configuration is a prerequisite for a reliable Continuous Delivery pipeline.

In a traditional IT organization, waiting for test, QA or acceptance environments is a frequent source of inefficiency in the traditional software delivery process. In addition, unanticipated configuration differences between environments result in deployment failures, unexpected application behavior and further delays to the delivery process.

In a Continuous Delivery organization, new environments for development or QA can be spun up automatically or at the click of a button. There are no service tickets, handoffs or manual configuration steps, resulting in a fast process with a high level of reliability and reproducibility. These self-service environments function as a foundation for the delivery pipeline to facilitate the flow of new features to production.

Infrastructure as a Service – Environments on demand

In a traditional environment, the set of available environments is fixed: Development, Test, Acceptance, Staging and Production. The servers in each environment are maintained by operations, with configuration changes applied manually via a formal change request process. Adding a new machine can take weeks or even months, as servers needs to be ordered, shipped and physically installed in the data center.

With Continuous Delivery, there is no concept of a fixed set of environments – they are created and destroyed on-the-fly, as needed. Provisioning of a new environment, based on one of many available templates, can be triggered automatically or via a self-service portal. The new virtual machines are ready for use within minutes, and can be automatically deprovisioned when no longer in use, maximizing resource efficiency and cost-effectiveness.

. The middleware on each machine is automatically installed and configured, and various sets of sample data are available for databases, including recent snapshots of the production DB. This allows teams to quickly and reliably reproduce production environments to try out new features or carry out tests.

Hands-off operations - "Zero Access Platform"

Traditionally, configuration of the IT infrastructure is handled manually by operations. Changes that developers make to their development machines to get applications to operate are often forgotten in deployment manuals, causing the configuration of the various environments to drift apart, resulting in unexpected failures. And there simply aren't enough system administrators to handle all the environment creation and configuration requests submitted by the development teams.

With Continuous Delivery, the IT infrastructure is managed according to a clear "hands-off" policy. Neither developers nor administrators are granted login access to the machines, except in production emergencies. The system and middleware configurations are specified by version-controlled blueprints that are applied and audited automatically by provisioning and configuration management tools.

If a configuration change needs to be made, an administrator updates the applicable blueprints for that server. The updates are checked into version control and picked up by the configuration management system, which calculates the required modifications and applies them to the target machines automatically. In addition, all servers are scanned at regular intervals to ensure compliance with applicable blueprints.

Machines and environments are fully reproducible: any server can be destroyed and recreated with the configuration settings it had at any point in time. In this way, a very small team of system administrators can scale to manage thousands of machines effectively.

Key learning points

In a Continuous Delivery organization, automated provisioning and configuration management enables the pipeline to deliver quickly and reliably.

- Self-service portals allow teams to create ready-to-use environments on demand.

- The installation and configuration of operating systems, middleware, networking etc. is fully automated.

- Changes to the configuration of machines are only carried out automatically, to ensure stability.

10

Release Coordination:
Orchestrating your Pipeline

In the previous chapter, we saw how automated
provisioning and configuration management enables the
pipeline to deliver quickly and reliably. In this chapter,
we show how the Continuous Delivery pipeline relates to
your existing release process.

In a traditional software delivery organization, releases are typically overseen by release managers. They are responsible for getting the entire team together to plan what needs to be done, coordinating and tracking all the activities across multiple teams as the release progresses, and report back to the business – inevitably, not frequently enough.

In a Continuous Delivery environment, dedicated release managers are seldom required: the delivery pipeline orchestrates the sequence of automated tasks that constitute the release process. The pipeline is the responsibility of the delivery team as a whole, including the business. Anyone can track the progress of a new application version at any time via the pipeline dashboards. In other words, the release process certainly still exists in a Continuous Delivery environment – in an entirely automated form, allowing many new application versions and features to be released extremely rapidly.

Pipeline Optimization

In a full Continuous Delivery pipeline, all activities in each stage, all approvals and all transitions between stages are automated. A developer checks a change to the source code into version control, the updated codebase is automatically build, unit- and integration tested, deployed to an acceptance test environment, acceptance tested, approved and deployed to production.

A basic pipeline starts with a simple, linear progression of automated stages. Every new application version progresses through these stages, passing a series of automated approval gates before deployment to production. Each approval is aimed at ensuring a different aspect of quality of the deliverable in order to prevent errors in production.

One immediate observation to be made about this simple pipeline is that it executes stages in sequence even when these stages are independent of each other. Provided sufficient execution capacity and a suitable target environment is available, pipeline throughput time can be improved by running such stages in parallel. In addition, work can also be parallelized *within* stages. For example, if automated acceptance tests can be run across four systems rather than one, the acceptance test stage can be completed in a quarter of the time.

From Release Plans to Delivery Pipelines

Release coordination tools allow you to take your current manual or partially automated release process, identify the biggest bottlenecks and delays through automated value stream mapping, and progressively replace these with automated tasks.

They can prove useful tools in the transition from your current process to a fully automated Continuous Delivery pipeline, helping you to deliver the greatest possible improvement and measure the benefits, at every step.

Key learning points

Continuous Delivery has a significant effect on the release process.

- Release managers no longer have to coordinate people and activities to deliver a new release to production.
- The release process is entirely automated and its progress can be tracked via a dashboard.
- You can optimize the release process by parallelizing different stages in the pipeline.
- A release coordination tool can help you move away from a traditional release process towards a continuous delivery process.

11

Dare to think differently

In the previous chapters, we saw how to speed up the time to market and improve the quality of the changes at the same time. In this chapter, we show how Continuous Delivery seriously alters the way you think about software development.

Once the building blocks to "deliver features better" are in place, you can start to take your Continuous Delivery process to the next level for "delivering *better* features better"!

With automated testing now as an integral part of your software delivery process, the quality level of your applications should be consistently high. However, if a new release does happen to behave unexpectedly, "rolling forward" to an improved version should be the default choice.

Rollbacks make sense if you deliver software in large, complex releases consisting of many changes in one big batch. In such cases, identifying which of the new features is responsible for any system instability is rarely possible. The only safe thing to do is to revert all your modifications.

In a Continuous Delivery environment where software is put into production feature by feature, the changes made to the system are much smaller. This makes it far easier for the development team to quickly create a new version that fixes or removes the troublesome feature and release it rapidly to your customers through the delivery pipeline: *Don't look back, roll forward*

Test in Production
The wide-ranging changes that are typical in "big bang" releases make it almost impossible to run new application versions silently in production, or expose this new application to only a subset of production users.

The increased risk associated with large, complex releases means that all aspects of the new application version need to be thoroughly tested in dedicated, production-like test and acceptance environments. Due to the associated cost, these environments are scarce and never quite production-like enough, leading to delays and expensive failures after a go-live.

In a Continuous Delivery organization, small, feature by feature changes and the high level of quality verified by the delivery pipeline mean deployments to production are a much more low-risk affair. The new application version can usually run alongside the existing system, exposed to only a limited group of "early access" users.

Expensive, dedicated production-like test environments can be eliminated and the false "but it worked in the acceptance environment!" sense of security can be avoided. There is no more reliable way to test a feature than running it in production.

Product teams, Devops & "Bizdevops"

In a typical organization, business, developers and operations work in typical silos in order to establish local optimizations. While this may increase the efficiency of one particular department, it often goes at great cost of end-to-end value chain efficiency. In the end, it basically reduces the ability of the company as a whole to effectively deliver customer value.

Effectiveness in terms of overall business value generated is more important than efficiency in terms of departmental cost. IT needs to be freed from its silo and need to become organized as an integral part of the business, typically as a multidisciplinary team focused on delivering benefits to the business – one of the core principles of Devops.

Integrated business, development and operations teams that are responsible for the end-to-end process of achieving a business goal will make more effective choices than segregated teams working to produce intermediate deliverables that are "thrown over the wall" into the next silo, without awareness of a common business goal.

In that sense, think not just Devops but "Bizdevops" and organize your teams around the common aim of business and customer value.

Ongoing customer conversation

Delivering features on a continuous basis dramatically changes the way you can engage with your customers to shape products and functionality together. With the ability to easily deploy changes to production, an ability that Continuous Delivery provides, trying out new features and improvements is simple.

You can expose new functionality to a limited set of users and track "hard" metrics such as revenue and conversion rates, as well as "soft" data such as feedback posted through, for example, social media channels.

The measurements will quickly tell you whether a new idea is profitable and favorably received. If customers do not react positively to the new functionality, you can rapidly initiate a "dialogue" with your user base to determine desired improvements and deliver these while developing an on-going "conversation" with your customers.

> ### Key learning points
> Continuous Delivery seriously alters the way you think about software development:
> - The default option of dealing with production issues is to deliver a new version instead of rolling back to a previous configuration.
> - Create teams that have full responsibility for the entire system and authorize them to continuously improve the business outcome.
> - Run real life tests in production and measure the effect of suggested improvements.
> - Shape the system together with your customers, by measuring the effect of new ideas in production.

12

Getting Started with Continuous Delivery

In the previous chapters, we saw the processes, practices and effects of Continuous Delivery and how it will alter the way you think about the software delivery process. In this chapter, we show you how to get started.

If you believe that there is room for improvement in your organization's software delivery process and you are interested in seeing how Continuous Delivery can help, the next step will be to figure out how to start turning your company into a Continuous Delivery organization.

Here, we give some advice on how to kick off that journey. However, keep in mind that realizing the full benefits of Continuous Delivery may require significant changes to your company's processes and attitudes.

Continuous Delivery is more than just introducing a few new tools. It affects your organizational structure, roles and responsibilities, how your developers go about their work and, ultimately, the relationship between IT and the business.
Turning your company into a Continuous Delivery organization will only succeed when the topic is approached in manageable steps.

Agile Development

Getting your development teams to work in an iterative manner is always a prerequisite for Continuous Delivery. If you have not yet adopted an agile methodology, this is an excellent first step. An agile mindset, focusing on business value and continuity through short, iterative development cycles, is a natural generator of the continuous flow of changes to production enabled by Continuous Delivery.

Acknowledging the Challenge

The greatest problem faced by a traditional software delivery organization is not the inefficient, error-prone delivery and feedback process as such. The biggest impediment is the acceptance that the current process represents the "natural order of things".

Acknowledging that your delivery process can be improved, and communicating clearly that the way things are currently done is open to debate and revision, is a critical prerequisite for a successful Continuous Delivery transformation.

Value Stream Mapping

In order to identify where the most immediate improvements are available, work with your delivery and business teams to map out your current value stream. A value stream describes all steps in a particular process, their duration and any intermediate idle time. In a typical software delivery process, you will find that a large proportion of the overall throughput time will be spent idling.

Having defined your value stream, you and the team can then determine where the most painful bottlenecks are and which improvements are likely to deliver the greatest benefit. Estimate the benefits in quantifiable terms such as cost, quality and time to market and start implementing those improvements that will give the biggest bang for the buck.

One Bottleneck at a Time

There is no such thing as a standard "Continuous Delivery Transformation Plan" suitable for every organization. However, a pattern common to successful implementations, is to favor incremental "biggest pain first" approaches over blanket, organization-wide roll-outs.

The decision to adopt Continuous Delivery itself will not magically solve all of your delivery problems. Implementing Continuous Delivery practices will however bring the biggest bottlenecks rapidly and clearly to light. And every time you eliminate the most painful bottleneck, the pipeline will quickly highlight the next challenging issue.

The result: a clear and measurable improvement path to delivering better features better through Continuous Delivery.

Key learning points

In order to implement Continuous Delivery in your organization:

- Adopt an agile method in your software development teams.
- Acknowledge the need for significant improvement of the current process.
- Create a value stream map of the software delivery process.
- Improve your process step by step, attacking the biggest bottlenecks first.

13

Final Thoughts

Complex, "big bang" releases, slow, error-prone manual processes, repeated handovers and delays lead to failures in production, poor quality and dissatisfied users. If a company wants to be remain ahead of its competitors, it needs to do better than that.

Release high-quality software straight to production and set up a rapid and effective feedback loop between your business and your users.

Start your path to Continuous Delivery now and experience the benefits of delivering business value in days, not months!

DOs and DON'Ts

It's worth repeating that there is no such thing as a standard "Continuous Delivery Transformation Plan" suitable for every organization. What we can put together though, is a set of practices and tools that are commonly found in successful Continuous Delivery implementations.

If one of the "DON'T" patterns sounds similar to what you're experiencing in your organization, it's worth investigating what kind of benefits the corresponding "DO" could deliver for you.

	DO	DON'T
1.	Minimal, automatically-verifiable specs	Overly complete, ambiguous requirements that require human translation or interpretation to be verified
2.	Continuous Integration	Long, isolated development efforts followed by "Merge Hell"
3.	Automated validation of executable specs	Test scenarios manually created by interpreting requirements, then manually executed
4.	Automated deployment	Hand-off and manual installation based on lengthy deployment manuals
5.	Automated provisioning and system configuration management	Manual creation and configuration of new target servers and environments
6.	Regular go-live of small code changes	Infrequent, stressful "big bang" releases containing lots of new features and fixes
7.	End-to-end delivery teams, including the business	Business "throws requirements over the wall" to IT
8.	Build up automated pipeline orchestration guided by metrics and value stream mapping	*Either* Spreadsheets and release plan documents *or* automation for the sake of automation, "because it's cool"

Glossary of Terms

A/B Testing

A technique in which a new feature, or different variants of a feature, are made available to different sets of users and evaluated by comparing metrics and user behaviour.

Acceptance Testing

Typically high-level testing of the entire system carried out to determine whether the overall quality of both new and existing features is good enough for the system to go to production.

Agile

A software development and, more broadly, business methodology that emphasizes short, iterative planning and development cycles to provide better control and predictability and support changing requirements as projects evolve.

Black box testing

A testing or quality assurance practice which assumes no knowledge of the inner workings of the system being tested, and which thus attempts to verify external rather than internal behaviour or state.

Build Automation

Tools or frameworks that allow source code to be automatically compiled into releasable binaries. Usually includes code-level unit testing to ensure individual pieces of code behave as expected.

Canary Release

A go-live strategy in which a new application version is released to a small subset of production servers and heavily monitored to determine whether it behaves as expected. If everything seems stable, the new version is rolled out to the entire production environment.

Continuous Delivery (CD)
Continuous Delivery is a set of processes and practices that radically removes waste from your software production process, enables faster delivery of high-quality functionality and sets up a rapid and effective feedback loop between your business and your users.

Continuous Integration (CI)
A development practice in which all changes by developers to a shared codebase are regularly combined (*integrated*) into a single version and tested, detecting errors and conflicts as soon as possible.

Dark Launch
A go-live strategy in which code implementing new features is released to a subset of the production environment but is not visibly, or only partially, activated. The code is exercised, however, in a production setting without users being affected by potential problems.

Delivery Pipeline
A sequence of orchestrated, automated tasks implementing the software delivery process for a new application version. Each step in the pipeline is intended to increase the level of confidence in the new version to the point where a go/no-go decision can be made. A delivery pipeline can be considered the result of optimizing an organization's software delivery process.

Deployment Automation a.k.a. Application Release Automation
Tools, scripts or products that automatically install and correctly configure a given version of an application in a target environment, ready for use.

DevOps

A type of organization or organizational mindset in which all teams participating in the service delivery process collaborate closely, focused on the common goal of providing value to the customer. A common misconception is that the approach is limited to developers and operations: it should include QA and the business, too.

Functional Testing

Testing of the end-to-end system to validate (new) functionality. With executable specifications, Functional Testing is carried out by running the specifications against the application.

Infrastructure as a Service (IaaS)

Cloud-hosted virtualized machines usually billed on a "pay as you go" basis. Users have full control of the machines but need to install and configure any required middleware and applications themselves.

Infrastructure as Code

A system configuration management technique in which machines, network devices, operating systems, middleware etc. are specified in a fully automatable format. The specification or "blueprint" is regarded as code that is executed by provisioning tools, kept in version control and generally subject to the same practices used for application code development.

Lean

"Lean manufacturing" or "lean production" is an approach or methodology that aims to reduce waste in production process by focussing on preserving value. Largely derived from practices developed by Toyata in car manufacturing, lean concepts have been applied to software development as part of agile methodologies.

The Value Stream Map (VSM), which attempts to visually identify valuable and wasteful process steps, is a key lean tool.

Non-functional Requirements (NFRs)

The specification of system qualities such as ease-of-use, clarity of design, latency, speed, ability to handle large numbers of users etc. that describe how easily or effectively a piece of functionality can be used, rather than simply whether it exists. These characteristics can also be addressed and improved using the Continuous Delivery feedback loop.

NoOps

A type of organization in which the management of systems on which applications run is either handled completely by an external party (such as a PaaS vendor) or fully automated. A NoOps organization aims to maintain little or no in-house operations capability or staff.

Pipeline Orchestration

Tools or products that enable the various automated tasks that make up a Continuous Delivery pipeline to be invoked at the right time. They generally also record the state and output of each of those tasks and visualize the flow of features through the pipeline.

Platform as a Service (PaaS)

Cloud-hosted application runtimes, usually billed on a "pay as you go" basis. Customers provide the application code and limited configuration settings, the middleware, databases etc. are part of the provided runtime.

Product Owner

A person or role responsible for the definition, prioritization and maintenance of the list of outstanding features and other work to be tackled by a development team. Product Owners are common in agile software development methodologies and often represent the business or customer organization. Product Owners need to play a more active, day-to-day role in the development process than their counterparts in more traditional software development processes.

Provisioning
The process of preparing new systems for users (in a Continuous Delivery scenario, typically development or test teams). The systems are generally virtualized and instantiated on demand. Configuration of the machines to install operating systems, middleware etc. is handled by automated system configuration management tools, which also verify that the desired configuration is maintained.

Regression Testing
Testing of the end-to-end system to verify that existing functionality has not been negatively impacted by changes to the application.

Release Coordination
The definition and execution of all the actions required to take a new feature or set of features from code check-in to go-live. In a Continuous Delivery environment, this is largely or entirely automated and carried out by the pipeline.

Test-Driven Development (TDD)
A development practice in which small tests to verify the behaviour of a piece of code are written *before the code itself.* The tests initially fail, and the aim of the developer(s) is then to add code to make them succeed.

Unit Testing

Code-level (does not require a fully installed end-to-end system to run) testing to verify the behaviour of individual pieces of code. Test Driven Development makes extensive use of unit tests to describe and verify intended behaviour.

Value Stream Mapping

A process visualization and improvement technique used heavily in lean manufacturing and engineering approaches. Value stream maps are used to identify essential process steps vs. "waste" that can be progressively eliminated from the process.

Virtualization

A systems management approach in which users and applications do not use physical machines, but simulated systems running on actual, "real" hardware. Such "virtual machines" can be automatically created, started, stopped, cloned and discarded in a matter of seconds, giving operations tremendous flexibility.

Waterfall

A software development methodology based on a phased approach to projects, from "Requirements Gathering" through "Development" etc. to "Release". Phases late in the process (typically related to testing and QA) tend to be squeezed as delays put projects under time pressure.

White box testing

A testing or quality assurance practice which is based on verifying the correct functioning of the internals of a system by examining its (internal) behaviour and state as it runs.

About the authors

Andrew Phillips is VP Product Management at XebiaLabs in Boston, USA. Andrew is a cloud, application delivery and automation expert and has been part of the shift to more automated application delivery platforms. He sits on expert panels and regularly speaks at conferences and meetups on DevOps and Continuous Delivery.

Michiel Sens is Principal Consultant at Xebia IT Architects in The Netherlands. Michiel specializes in Continuous Delivery and full lifecycle software development programs. He advocates the use of Continuous Delivery at seminars and meetups, while remaining in touch with its details by performing actual implementations as well.

Adriaan de Jonge is Principal Consultant at Xebia IT Architects in The Netherlands. Adriaan specializes in Lean and Continuous Delivery. Before this book, he wrote two developer's guides on web technology, published by Addison-Wesley in 2011 and 2012.

Mark van Holsteijn is Principal Consultant for Xebia IT Architects in The Netherlands. Mark specializes in Continuous Delivery and Automated Provisioning. He pioneered in the field of Automated Deployment and Provisioning and designed and implemented the Kadaster success story.

CONTINUOUS DELIVERY:
REMOVE WASTE FROM YOUR SOFTWARE DELIVERY PROCESS

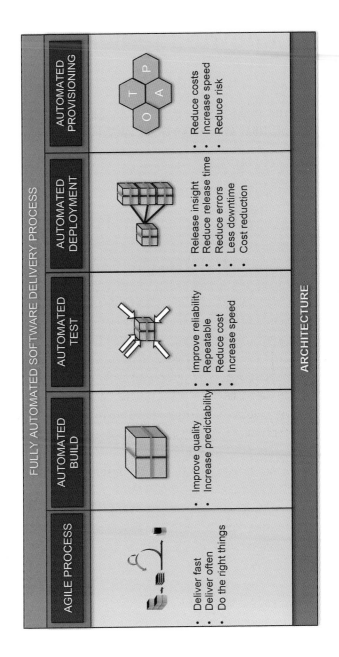

FULLY AUTOMATED SOFTWARE DELIVERY PROCESS

AGILE PROCESS
- Deliver fast
- Deliver often
- Do the right things

AUTOMATED BUILD
- Improve quality
- Increase predictability

AUTOMATED TEST
- Improve reliability
- Repeatable
- Reduce cost
- Increase speed

AUTOMATED DEPLOYMENT
- Release insight
- Reduce release time
- Reduce errors
- Less downtime
- Cost reduction

AUTOMATED PROVISIONING
- Reduce costs
- Increase speed
- Reduce risk

ARCHITECTURE

Acknowledgements

This book is the result of the efforts of many people. The knowledge in this book is based not only on our own experience, but also on that of many colleagues inside and outside Xebia and XebiaLabs. We acknowledge the contributions of everybody who shared their knowledge with us and gave valuable feedback on early revisions.

Within Xebia, every colleague who has shared knowledge and experience on Continuous Delivery has contributed to our knowledge and therefore to this book.

Beyond Xebia, we owe thanks to Dave Farley and Jez Humble from ThoughtWorks for their excellent technical book, *Continuous Delivery*. And we particularly thank Dave Farley for reviewing our book and contributing a foreword.

We are grateful to Jeff Sutherland for his foreword for this book and for his achievements in making Agile processes popular throughout the world of IT.

We thank our reviewers for their constructive feedback and excellent advice: Coert Baart, Heather Sill Moses and TJ Randall from XebiaLabs, Enrique Zschuschen, Martin van Steenis and Reinier Verschure from Xebia.

We owe a big thank you to our marketing department, Petra Kiers, Lianne Verhoeven and Lotte Schram for their efforts in finding a publisher and planning promotional activities around this book.

We are grateful to our publisher, Leo Klaver from Tiem Publishing for his and their professional handling of this book, and for expert "tips & tricks" that provided the finishing touches.

Last but not least, we thank our managing director Guido Schoonheim, who ably fulfilled the role of executive editor. The book you are reading would not exist were it not for his guidance, direction and motivation throughout the writing and editing process.